Stay Strong and Other Useless Words

OrangeBooks Publication

1st Floor, Rajhans Arcade, Mall Road, Kohka, Bhilai, Chhattisgarh 490020
Website: **www.orangebooks.in**

First Edition, 2025

ISBN: 978-93-6554-633-0

Price: Rs. 249.00

Printed in India

STAY STRONG AND OTHER USELESS WORDS

NIKHIL KUNCHE

Orange Books Publication
www.orangebooks.in

Preface

I used to think there was time. Time to say things. Time to fix things. Time to plan better. I thought life gives warnings. That when something terrible is about to happen, it announces itself like a storm. I kept saying I'll do this tomorrow, I'll take care of that next week. I kept waiting for a perfect moment to act, to be there more, to show up better. I told myself that I'm buying time, not wasting it.

I ignored the warning signs. All of them. I kept saying it's nothing. Just a phase. A complication, maybe, but we'll get through it. I had this arrogant belief that I would save her. That I could figure it all out, talk to the right doctors, research the right things, fast for her, pray for her, protect her like I always thought I would. I was so sure that no matter how bad it looked, she would come back home. That she would sit on her couch again. That I would make her coffee. That we'd laugh at the same stupid cat videos. That we'd watch another movie together while eating something we both loved. I kept visualizing it. I clung to it. I told myself again and again, this is temporary. She's going to be fine.

But she never came home.

That sentence alone has destroyed me more than anything else in this world. She never came home. Every day now is a punishment for believing there was more time. I don't know how to carry this. I don't know why I'm still here. I don't know what I'm supposed to do with these meals, these mornings, this breath. She trusted me with her life, and I couldn't save her. I lost her right in front of my eyes, and the world kept moving like nothing happened.

I didn't write this book to cope. I wrote it because I couldn't stop myself from falling apart. There was no plan. These words are what came out of a son who couldn't keep his promise. I was supposed to protect her. She died believing I would.

This book is not a tribute. It's a breakdown that never ended.

- Nikhil Kunche

Contents

Chapter - 1

Stay Strong

I don't remember the person's face.

But I can still hear the words.

They came at me before I could even understand what had just happened. Before my body could decide if it was going to cry or collapse, someone came up and said it like they were offering me a tissue after a small accident. 'Stay strong, Nikhil.' As if I were doing something wrong by standing there, frozen, my mind still stuck in that ICU where my mother had just left me.

I can still feel her hand in mine. Still warm. Still soft. Still hers. My mother wasn't just a mother. She was the reason I could face the world outside without falling apart. She was my anchor, my strength, my safe place. And now the world was demanding me to 'stay strong' in the exact moment when the only person who made me strong had gone.

Nobody cared about what was happening inside me.

They only cared about their comfort, about keeping the flow of events moving smoothly. There were guests to handle, people to inform, rituals to arrange, and logistics to check. They didn't want the scene disturbed by the messy business of grief. 'Stay strong' wasn't for me. It was for them. To keep them from feeling the discomfort of seeing a son lose his mother. They needed the world to look normal, the photos to be taken, the timelines to be followed.

'Stay strong' is a phrase that hides its violence in politeness. What it really says is, stop. Hide it. We don't want to see you collapse. Keep your grief invisible. Make yourself palatable. Act like the strong son they all expect you to be.

'Stay strong, ' the first time I heard it, it wasn't in the ICU. It was two hours later, in the underground parking lot of the hospital. They made us wait there, like criminals, while they processed the 'discharge formalities' of my mother. Can you imagine that? Processing the body of a sitting Justice like she was a file that needed closing. Two hours. Two hours of standing in that suffocating parking lot, where the stench of death mixed with exhaust fumes and the silence of people too embarrassed to look me in the eye.

And then they brought her down. Wrapped in a white cloth. With a label on top.

A label.

Like she was an object to be transported.

Like she wasn't the woman who had police escorts, gunmen, courtrooms waiting for her orders, thousands of lives she had touched, cases she had fought for, people she had defended. She was my mother. She was Justice M.G. Priyadarsini. And now she was lying there, voiceless, faceless, reduced to a stretcher being rolled out by strangers.

That was the first time I collapsed. My knees gave way. I fell right there, on the cold cement of the parking lot, in front of all those people who wanted me to 'stay strong.' I couldn't. I didn't. I didn't care. My world had just been pulled out from under me, and I refused to pretend otherwise.

But even as I cried, even as I howled like an animal, they kept saying it. 'Stay strong, Nikhil.' Like it was a command, like they were shoving a mask onto my face while my soul was bleeding out. 'Stay strong' is not comfort. It's a prison sentence. It's society demanding that you act like the son of a Justice, that you carry the family name with dignity, that you suppress the most honest thing you'll ever feel in your life.

But I failed them. I broke down. And I'm not sorry for it.

Sometimes, I sit in the dark and wonder what she would have done if I were the one lying dead. If I were the one stretched out, lifeless, with a label slapped on my chest, being pushed around like a discarded package. I know the answer. She wouldn't have 'stayed strong.' She wouldn't have let them take me like that. She would have broken the world apart if she had to. She would have clung to my body, screamed until the walls cracked. She would have shaken the heavens. She would have thrown herself on the floor, cursed the gods, cursed the doctors, cursed herself. She wouldn't have cared about what people expected of her. She never lived for people.

And yet, when it was her, they expected me to do what she never would have done if it were me. They expected me to swallow it, stand straight, bow politely, nod at guests, and act like the dignified son of a dignified judge. But my mother never taught me to live like that. She never taught me to hide my tears. She told me to feel everything. To fight when something wasn't right. To stand up even if the world laughed. She was the only one who permitted me to be human.

And now these strangers, these parasites in the garb of well-wishers, want me to dishonour everything she taught me by performing their script of 'strength'? By wiping my tears in front of them, smiling like I'm, okay? She would have hated that. She would have slapped anyone who told her to 'stay strong' if I had died. She would have burned the world down. And now, without her, they expect me to play nice, to be quiet, to 'move on.'

No. She wouldn't have stayed strong. She would have grieved me like a mother who lost her only child. And that's exactly what I want to do for her. The way she deserved to be mourned.

I wish it were me instead of her. I wish whatever years are left in my life could have been given to her, that I could have disappeared quietly if it meant she would live longer, serve longer, continue bringing justice to people who needed her more than the world will ever need someone like me. She was a pillar of justice. A protector. A warrior. The world is emptier now that she's gone. And I hate that I'm the one left behind.

When they brought her home, everything was arranged as if it were a celebration. They cleaned the house. They decorated the floors with flowers, lit lamps, and set up the stage for the final rituals. The priests arrived like event managers, setting up their space, adjusting the photo, and preparing the chants. And all I could see was the absurdity of it. They wanted her to look peaceful, wanted the room to smell of incense. But there was nothing peaceful about it. Nothing holy. It was all makeup on a wound that refused to heal. They dressed her in her best saree. They combed her hair. They placed garlands on her. They tried to paint a smile on death, to hide the horror that lived underneath the flowers and prayers. They wanted it to look like a beautiful goodbye. But it wasn't. It was violent. It was cruel. It was an act staged for the living to pretend they can handle something they can't.

The same sickness as 'Stay strong.' Hide the truth. Erase the mess. Don't let the rawness of grief show in public. Make it look graceful, controlled, holy. They wanted me to sit there, fold my hands, receive people with a smile, pretend like I'm okay. But I couldn't. I sat there, breathing through rage, through heartbreak, through the smell of the incense that now makes me want to vomit.

No one talks about the violence of how they make the dead look 'peaceful.' How they force the living to act like nothing broke. How they dress it all up with rituals and chants and call it closure. It wasn't closure. It was a lie. A performance for the comfort of others. And I hated every second of it.

They kept saying it. Over and over. As if the phrase itself could rebuild the ruins of my life. 'Stay strong, Nikhil.' 'She wouldn't want to see you like this.' 'You have to be brave.' Brave for whom? Brave for what? They didn't understand that when she died, it wasn't just my mother who left. It was the entire universe I had built around her. The routines, the reasons, the invisible scaffolding that held me up, all of it crumbled in one cruel moment.

They spoke as if strength were some kind of a backup generator you could switch on when the main power fails. As if you could stand on the debris of your life and smile like nothing happened. But there was nothing left inside me to power up. Only wreckage. Only a hollow, aching hole where everything once was.

They said it because it made them feel better. Because if I collapsed in front of them, it would remind them that they are just as breakable, that their families are just as mortal. That their smiles, their prayers, their rituals, none of it can save them when death decides to knock on their door. That's why they needed me to play strong. To perform it like an obedient actor in their play.

But I couldn't. I wouldn't. Because to pretend would be to dishonor everything she was. She never faked strength. She fought for it. She lived it. And if I have to fall to the floor, scream, curse the gods, break plates, punch walls, I will. Because that is the only honest thing left in a world that collapsed the moment she left it.

When we brought my mother home, I thought that was the end of it. I thought I would get some time to sit with her, to be near her, even if she was no longer breathing. But the world didn't give me that time. Before I could even process that she was lying there, inside that brutal glass box in the middle of our hall, my father collapsed. His body gave up. His mind couldn't take it anymore. My brother and I had to leave her there, leave her alone, and rush him to the hospital.

There was this one moment, just one, when I looked at him lying in that hospital bed, the machines hooked to him, his face grey, hollow, almost unrecognizable, and I thought, 'I have lost both my parents in the same day.' That's how bad it was. That's how fragile everything became in an instant.

I can't blame him. I won't. He was with her every second. He never left her side. No sleep. No food. No breaks. He stood by her in ways I didn't even know love could exist. I saw a side of him that made me believe maybe, just maybe, someone could love another person so completely, so painfully, that when they leave, your whole-body collapses. I can admit it now; he might have loved her even more than I did.

We didn't have time to feel sorry for ourselves. There was no space to cry, to break, to grieve. My brother and I were stuck between two disasters, our mother at home in that glass box, our father in a hospital bed, running between them, trying to keep both worlds from falling apart completely.

And while all of this was happening, the people I thought would be there? They weren't. My so-called best friends, my so-called family friends, the people who sat in our home, laughed with us, joked with us, shared meals with us, all of them disappeared. Not even a call. Not even a text. They left us to crumble on our own.

And while all of this was happening, the people I thought would be there? They weren't. My so called best friends, the ones who had laughed in our living room, shared meals with us, vanished. Not even a message. Not even a call. But in that darkness, the most unexpected people showed up. Quiet faces who didn't flinch at the horror, who didn't ask what needed to be done, they just did it. Friends who didn't preach or perform, who didn't pity, but simply stood beside us when the whole world stepped away. I don't know what would have happened to us if not for them. If you're reading this, you know who you are. And whatever is left of me, thank you.

Chapter - 2

She Is at A Better Place Now

I don't remember the face.

But I remember the words.

'She's at a better place now, Nikhil.'

They said it like it was a band-aid for a bullet wound. Like it was supposed to fix everything. But it didn't. It made everything worse.

It happened at home, right after we brought her back. She was lying there, inside that brutal glass box in the center of the hall. The house was crowded. People coming and going. Some with folded hands. Some with plastic tears that dried up the second they walked outside. And then someone walked up to me. Placed their hand on my shoulder, as if they were offering me wisdom. As if they understood anything about what was happening to me. And they said it.

'She's at a better place now.'

I can still feel my stomach twist. I can still taste the bile in my throat. My mother was right there. I could see her face through the glass. The woman who raised me, loved me, protected me, and fought for me. And they had the nerve to stand in my house and tell me she was in a better place? What place? Where? What world exists that deserves her more than this one? More than this house? More than this family?

They said it like they were handing me a blanket, like it was supposed to comfort me. But it suffocated me. It tasted like dirt. Like they were burying her with their words before we even had the chance to say goodbye. I wanted to scream at them. I wanted to shove their comfort down their throats and tell them to never say those words again. But I couldn't. I couldn't even breathe properly. I stood there, silent, choking on the rage that filled my chest.

It wasn't just the words. It was what they meant. They didn't say it for me. They didn't say it for her. They said it for themselves. So, they could escape the discomfort of facing me, of facing the reality of what was in front of them. So, they could put a ribbon on death and move on, satisfied that they said something 'kind.'

But it wasn't kind. It was cruel. It was violent. It was a lie. My mother's place was here. In this house. In this life. In this world. And no god, no heaven, no fantasy land could ever be better than that. They stripped her of everything she built, everything she loved, and then tried to decorate it with their hollow words.

That was the first time I realised, they say 'She's at a better place now, not because they care, but because they're scared. Because they can't handle the truth. That she's gone. And nothing they say will ever make that okay.

Who gets to decide what is a better place?

Who gave them the authority to declare that she is somewhere better now?

They say it like they've been there, like they've walked its streets, spoken to its gods, tasted its air. But they haven't. They're just repeating phrases they've heard at other funerals, phrases designed to make themselves feel better, not me. Not us.

Would my mother have called it a better place? No. She wouldn't have. She would have fought to stay right here. She did fight. She fought every day for one more moment in this world, in this house, with her family, with the work she loved, the people who looked up to her. She didn't want a better place in the sky. She wanted this place. This life. This family. This broken, chaotic, human world. This was her world.

But they can't handle that truth. They can't handle the ugliness of death. They can't handle the silence she left behind. So, they create these fantasies, these fairy tales about better places and peaceful journeys and god's plans. They talk about death like it's some grand promotion. Like, she got transferred to a better city. A better court. A better assignment. They say. But death is not better. It's nothingness. absence. It's the silence of her empty chair. It's the fading scent of her room.

And even if there was a better place, it wasn't hers. She belonged here. With us. With me. In this mess of a world that needed her more than any make-believe heaven ever could. They didn't say it for her. They said it for themselves. Because they were too scared to sit in the same room as my grief and admit that maybe, just maybe, there is no better place.

Chapter - 3
Time Heals All Wounds

It didn't take long for people to start expecting me to heal. They didn't say it outright, but I could feel it in their tone, in the way they looked at me, in how their words started changing. They didn't ask how I was doing because they genuinely cared. They asked so they could reassure themselves that I was "getting better." As if grief had a calendar. As if by Day 10, I was supposed to start accepting things. As if by Day 15, I should be showing signs of "coping."

They never asked if I was still waking up in the middle of the night, hearing her voice. Or if I still walked into her room expecting to see her getting ready for court. They assumed time was some sort of medicine and that all I had to do was wait long enough and I'd be fine. But I wasn't healing. I wasn't even adjusting. I was standing still while the world started expecting movement from me.

I wasn't moving forward. I was being forced to function. They wanted me to eat like before, talk like before, respond to their messages like before. It wasn't about me. It was about them. It was about making sure my grief didn't last long enough to inconvenience their routines.

Time doesn't heal anything. It just creates a distance between the moment you last held them and the moment you realise you never will again. It doesn't soothe. It erodes. I'm not healing. I'm forgetting. Her laugh is getting harder to summon. The sound of her walking around the house, her keys, her voice, the exact way she said my name. These are the things time takes. And they dare to call that progress.

Every day, I am pushed further away from her, and they think that's recovery. But I'm not recovering. I'm decaying in silence while everyone else wants to believe that I'm getting better.

Time hasn't healed anything. It hasn't taught me how to cope. It hasn't made me stronger. All it has done is push her further away from me. Every hour that passes is another hour since she was last alive in this world. Every day that moves forward just makes the silence heavier. People call that healing. I call it erosion.

I've been looking at her phone. Her WhatsApp. Her groups. Our family groups. The High Court groups. Her friends' circles. It hasn't even been two full weeks. And already, they've replaced her. Her photo was the group display picture for a while. Now it's gone. People are sharing jokes again. Talking about politics. Sending good morning messages like nothing ever happened. It feels like she was a status they reacted to and then scrolled past.

These are the same people who stood in our house saying big words like "We're always here for you" and "You're not alone." They said it with trembling voices, with folded hands, with performative grief in their eyes. And then they left. I haven't seen them since. They returned to their routines. They had their tea, their court hearings, their jokes, and their shopping plans. They slipped back into life without hesitation.

And I'm still here. Sitting in the same spot where she used to sit. Breathing in the air she used to breathe. Trying to hold on to something that's fading more every day. And it makes me sick. To know that I'm the only one still here while they've all walked away, like she was a two-minute silence they were forced to observe.

They told me to stay strong. But not because they cared. They told me to stay strong so they could move on with a clean conscience. They didn't mean those words. They didn't mean any of it. It was noise. Empty, social noise that people make to avoid feeling anything real.

Time hasn't made anything better. It has just shown me how alone I really am.

I don't know what people mean when they say, "It will get better with time." Better in what way? Does breathing become easier? Does the absence become softer? Because it hasn't. Every day that moves forward feels like a betrayal. Not healing. Just abandonment that unfolds slowly. Quietly. Without warning.

They say time helps you adjust. What I feel instead is distance. Unwanted distance. Between me and the last time I touched her. The last time I saw her walk into a room. The last time she called my name. And each new day pushes that memory further into a space where it starts to lose definition. And that scares me more than anything. Because I know what comes next. The forgetting. Not all at once. Just piece by piece. Her exact voice. Her walk. Her favourite lines. Her cough. It all gets softer, and not in a comforting way. In a way that erases.

What hurts the most is not just that she's gone. It's that the world kept moving. The house got quiet. The trays of food stopped arriving. People stopped calling. The people who claimed to care vanished. Nobody asks how we are anymore. The rituals are done, and so they believe the grief is done too. They came. They cried. They left. Now we are alone in the wreckage.

I didn't choose to move on. I didn't want to. But time doesn't ask. It just drags you forward. Through hours. Through the days. Through dates you don't want to live through. And now every time I look at a calendar, I feel like I've betrayed her just by existing in a world she no longer belongs to.

Every day that I survive is a day she didn't get. And I'm supposed to pretend like these days are a gift. Like they're meaningful. But I don't want them. I want the life we had. The normalcy we didn't even know was precious. I want to hear her voice in the hallway. I want her presence at the dining table. I want the version of life where she existed.

Time hasn't healed anything. It has just emptied the rooms a little more. It has made the silence more permanent. And I hate that everyone else seems okay with that.

For a few days, the house was full. People moving in and out. Some cried loudly. Some cried quietly. Some didn't cry at all, but made sure to stand close enough to be noticed. There were garlands, flowers, trays of food, neighbours whispering instructions, relatives managing logistics like it was a wedding. None of it made sense to me. I didn't ask for it. I didn't care for it. But at least the house was not silent.

Then the silence came. Slowly, like a smell that doesn't go away. People started leaving. The lights were switched off. The leftover tea was thrown out. Plates disappeared from the kitchen sink. One by one, their cars backed out of the gate and drove away. And what was left behind was the kind of silence that doesn't feel peaceful. It feels abandoned. Heavy. Rotten.

The people who had held my shoulder and said, "We are always here for you" — they vanished. No follow-up messages. No calls. Not even a simple check-in. And these were not strangers. These were people who had stood near her body just a few days ago, looking serious, saying words like "unimaginable loss" and "anything you need." They said the lines. Then they left.

What stayed behind was a house that no longer made sense. Her chair. Her shoes were near the door. Her books are on the table. Her scent was fading room by room. And I, standing in it, waiting for someone to return. Not to talk. Just to acknowledge what was gone. But no one came back. And that's when I realized they were never really there. They showed up because that's what people do. They stood beside us because it was expected. And the moment those expectations ended, they returned to their lives.

The silence that stayed wasn't peaceful. It was mocking. It reminded me every second that the world had moved on, while I was still standing in the middle of what felt like a bomb site.

They all left. Only silence stayed. And it feels more honest than all their words put together.

Chapter - 4

She Wouldn't Want to See You Like This

I don't even remember who said it first. "She wouldn't want to see you like this." Maybe it was her friend. Maybe someone from the court. Maybe a distant relative who barely ever spoke to her. They all started saying it like they knew her, like they had some sacred insight into what she would have thought about the way I was distressed.

I was still frozen. Still trying to make sense of the fact that she was gone. Still watching her photo on the wall like she would step out of it if I stared long enough. And suddenly, my pain became a problem. Not because it was hurting me, but because it was making them uncomfortable.

They didn't say it because they understood what she meant to me. They said it because they needed to push my pain back into a socially acceptable shape. Because my silence, my breakdowns, my inability to talk, made them feel something they didn't want to feel. And instead of staying with that discomfort, they weaponized her memory.

They used her name to shut me up. They used her name to make me feel guilty. And what angers me most is that they did it so easily. They took the person I loved more than anything and turned her into a tool. A script. A way to make themselves feel like they were being wise, like they were guiding me toward something noble.

But none of them knew her like I did. She wasn't a slogan. She was human. And she would have hated to see them use her name to police my emotions.

They always begin with praise. "She loved you more than anything." "You were her whole world." "She was proud of you." And every word of that is true. But what comes next is not. They take those facts and turn them into rules. They use her love for me as a reason why I should not break.

They say things like, "Be the son she raised you to be." "Stay strong in her memory." "She gave you everything. Now carry it forward." As if my emotions need to be filtered through some public image of strength. As if I am expected to stand tall, look composed, and make everyone around me comfortable just because she once smiled when she looked at me.

What they do is take the love between a mother and a son and twist it into a performance. They want me to wear her pride like armor. To show up, function, and move through this world like nothing happened. They say I should do it to honor her. But I know what she would have said if she saw me right now.

She would not ask me to hold back. She would not want me to shrink into silence. She would not want me to feel ashamed for being lost. If she were here, she would have sat beside me, without asking questions. She would have touched my head, let me cry, and told me not to worry about what the world expects.

But now that she is not with us, everyone else wants to decide how I should carry the weight she left behind. They speak in her name, but they do it for themselves. My pain unsettles them. My collapse makes them nervous. So, they hide behind her memory and try to instruct me with it.

She gave me strength, but she never made it a condition. She never asked me to pretend. And she never gave anyone else the right to use her love to shame me for feeling exactly how I feel.

If she could see what people have done in her name, she would cry.

Not because I'm broken. Not because I'm silent or angry or distant. But because of how they've used her absence. Because of how they've turned her into something she never was.

They talk about her with such confidence. They say she was strong, dignified, and graceful. They say she always wanted the best for everyone. They say she raised me to be composed, responsible, and collected. And maybe some of that is true. But the way they use those words now feels like theft.

They've taken her memory and wrapped it in instructions. They say, "You have to be strong like her," or "She wouldn't want to see you like this." And when they say that, they aren't honoring her. They're rewriting her. They're turning her into a tool to silence me. A script. A moral lesson.

If she saw what I've been made to carry in her name, she wouldn't stay quiet. She would be furious. Not at me. At them. She would never want her death to become a stage. She would never want her son to be paraded as a symbol of strength, while he silently falls apart in corners no one sees.

Chapter - 5

Life Must Go On

They didn't even wait.

The ceremonies had barely ended. Her scent still lingered in the room. Her slippers were still placed near the bed. Her phone still had unread messages. But people had already started saying it. Life must go on. As if that line could hold the weight of what had just happened.

Nobody asked me if I wanted to go on. Nobody asked if I had any reason to. They assumed I would return to routine. That I would function. That I would recover. As if survival were automatic. As if continuing to eat and speak and walk somehow proved that I was okay.

But I wasn't. I still am not. My life was built around her. My day had rhythm because she was part of it. My effort had meaning because she was watching. Everything I worked for had her at the centre. And when she left, the foundation cracked. Nothing made sense after that.

They didn't see that part. They only saw whether I was replying to messages. Whether I was eating. Whether I was showing signs of recovery. They needed signs. They needed to believe that I was adjusting. Because if I weren't, they would have to sit with the thought that nothing can truly protect us. That their world could break too.

So, they said it. Life must go on. They said it was not to support me, but to comfort themselves. It permitted them to stop thinking about what I was going through. To leave the house and resume their own lives. To convince themselves that I would eventually find a way to continue.

But I didn't want to continue. I wasn't even present. I just hadn't stopped breathing yet. That isn't a strength. That's just what happens when you're forced to remain alive after the reason you lived is no longer there.

The world kept moving. But I didn't.

They don't care if I'm okay. They just care if I'm operational.

From the outside, it looks like concern. Messages. Phone calls. Questions like "How are you holding up?" But the moment I pause, or the moment I hesitate, I can sense it. They want a simple answer. Something that closes the loop. Something that lets them feel like I'm on my way to being fine.

They're not really asking. They're hoping I say something that makes them feel useful. Something that lets them go back to their day with the belief that I'm stabilizing.

But I'm not stabilizing. I'm just responding. Because it's easier to say "yes" than to explain what's actually going on. It's easier to keep the conversation light than to carry the burden of their silence when I say something real.

What they want is proof that I'm returning to normal. That I've re-entered the cycle. That I'm working, replying, talking, and making decisions. That I'm ticking boxes. They want evidence that I'm functioning. Not true. Not reality. Just signs.

But I'm not a sign. I'm not a status update. I'm a person who lost the only person who made life meaningful. And that kind of pain doesn't come with polite answers or clean routines.

Sometimes I wake up and forget where I am. Sometimes I don't talk to anyone all day. Sometimes I eat because someone insists. Sometimes I don't. I'm not on a path. I'm not healing. I'm not moving forward. I'm just existing. And I don't owe them a performance.

But still, I give short replies. I say "yes, I'm managing" even when I'm not. Not because I'm pretending. But because I know they won't know what to do if I say anything else. They won't sit in the silence. They won't follow me into the depths of it. They'll back away. They'll change the subject. And I'll be left cleaning up their discomfort, along with my own.

So, I keep it brief. Not to protect myself. To protect them.

Everyone keeps saying it's a good sign that I'm able to "handle things."

They look at me and see that I'm eating again, speaking again, replying to people, walking into rooms. They take all of that as proof. Proof that I'm making progress. That I'm on the path toward normal.

But what they don't understand is that none of these actions mean anything. I don't do them because I've recovered. I do them because I have no other option. Because the world will not stop for me. Because if I don't keep moving, people will start calling again, asking again, showing up again, trying to fix what cannot be fixed.

This is not recovery. It is compliance. I follow the rhythm of the day because that's what is expected of me. Not because I believe in it. Not because I care. Most of the time, I don't even feel like I'm part of my body. I just do what the day demands.

They treat it like a success. They say I'm being strong. They smile when I speak. They act like I'm getting better. But I'm not getting better. I'm getting quieter. I'm getting tired. I am slowly running out of space inside me to even react.

What they call strength feels like punishment. Every task I complete feels like I'm betraying her memory. Like I'm moving further away from the last day she was alive. Like I'm participating in a life that no longer has her in it.

But the alternative is worse. If I stop responding, they panic. If I don't pick up the phone, they think something is wrong. If I tell them how I really feel, they either disappear or start giving advice I didn't ask for.

So, I continue. Not because I am strong. Not because I am healing. But because it is easier to follow the script than to sit with the silence that no one else wants to hear.

Chapter - 6

It Is God's Will

I heard it within the first hour.

Someone walked in, glanced at her body, folded their hands, turned to me and said, "It's God's will." As if that explained everything. As if those three words had the power to wipe away the wreckage that had just torn through my life.

God's will. That's what they said when they didn't know what else to say. That's what they said when they wanted the moment to feel sacred instead of unbearable. That's what they said when they needed the pain to have a purpose, because the idea that this was meaningless was too much for them to carry.

But I'm the one who has to carry it. Not them. Not God.

I watched her suffer. I watched her fight. I watched her breathe through pain and answer the questions of doctors while barely able to sit up. I watched her hold my hand through her fear, not knowing what was happening inside her own body. I watched every moment. Not some invisible force. And when she finally left, there was nothing divine in the room. No light. No angels. Just silence.

So don't talk to me about God's will.

What kind of will is this? What kind of God decides to take someone who spent her life defending the weak, upholding justice, and protecting her family, while so many cruel, empty people walk free, untouched, laughing, living, posting selfies? What exactly did she do wrong to be chosen for this plan?

They say it to protect themselves. That's what I've realised. Saying "it's God's will" allows them to retreat. It gives them emotional closure without having to actually confront anything. They don't want to sit in helplessness. They don't want to admit that sometimes, things are just cruel and undeserved and senseless. So, they wrap it in divinity and call it peace.

But for me, it's not peace. It's violence. That phrase is violence. It demands obedience. It tells me I am not allowed to scream. Not allowed to break. Not allowed to ask why. I'm supposed to fold my hands and whisper back, "Yes, it was God's will," while everything in me is being torn apart.

And the worst part is, they expect gratitude. They expect you to smile weakly and agree. Because if you don't, if you ask the real questions, if you express the rage, they look at you like you're faithless. Like you're disturbing their little temple of meaning.

But I'm not interested in their meaning. I'm not interested in their logic. I lost my mother. I watched her go. And I will not let anyone dress that up in cosmic poetry.

If this was God's will, then I want to know what kind of God this is.

Because I didn't just pray. I didn't just light a lamp and walk away. I gave everything I had. I sacrificed my body, my energy, my food, my hair, my beliefs, my dignity. I begged. I made deals. I fasted until my bones hurt. I walked barefoot. I stayed up entire nights reciting verses I didn't even believe in, because I was willing to do anything if it meant I could save her.

But they say it was God's will.

If that's true, then what kind of God ignores all of that?

For months, I barely ate. I fasted 25 days out of every 30. Sometimes even more. Not for fitness. Not for detox. I lied to people and told them it was for autophagy, for insulin resistance, for health. But I was starving myself because I thought maybe, just maybe, my hunger would turn into grace. That my pain would count for something.

I did every fast I could think of. All four Navratris. Ramzan. Christian fasts (I didn't even know the name), but I still followed it, thinking maybe their God listens better than mine. I honoured them all. Ayyappa, Tirupati Balaji, Shiva, Durga, Odin, the old gods, the new ones, even the ones I wasn't sure I believed in. I didn't care. I just wanted one of them to listen.

I was living off biryani and junk food before all this. And suddenly I was starving. And nobody saw the shift, because I hid it. Because I didn't want to be seen as desperate. But I was. I was desperate in a way that tears skin. I was willing to die slowly if it meant she would live.

I took vows. I said if she moved out of the ICU, I would walk barefoot up to Tirumala and shave off the 15 inches of hair I had spent years growing. If her blood gases stabilized, I would take up Ayyappa Deeksha and go to Sabarimala. I linked every improvement in her condition to a promise. A deal with God. I stacked them on top of each other until my entire life was one long prayer.

I fed thousands of people in Odin's name. Every Wednesday, without fail. I prayed to his ravens, Muninn and Huginn. I whispered to the gods of memory and thought. I lit incense. I fasted. I waited. I kept hoping.

And none of them came.

She still died.

And now they say it was God's will. No. That is not something I can accept. If this is divine, then this divinity is blind, deaf, and cruel. Because I begged on my knees. I offered everything. And what I got in return was silence.

And now, even food feels like betrayal. Every plate I sit in front of feels like a punishment. Because food was our thing. Mom and I used to sit together, watch food videos, send reels to each other, and plan what to teach the cook next. The last message she ever sent me on WhatsApp was a YouTube short, a dish she wanted to eat with me. She said, "When I come home, we'll eat this," with a thumbs - up emoji.

She never came home after that.

Now I place a plate in front of her photo and serve it to her like she's still here. I eat quietly. I bite through the food and the tears together. I swallow it all. Because I can't afford to break in front of my dad and brother. They're already destroyed.

Even cat videos have become weapons. I still share them on her Instagram account by reflex. Then I remember. Then I break again. All the things we saved, all the movies I didn't watch because I wanted to watch them with her. Now I can't watch anything. I can't sit through a Telugu movie without breaking. We used to watch something together every evening after she came from court. It was our ritual. Now it's gone.

And now you expect me to believe that some divine must have planned this? That all of this pain is part of a holy structure? I reject it. I spit on it. No God who takes everything and gives nothing deserves my reverence.

They keep telling me she's still here. That she's watching over me. That she hasn't really gone, she's just taken a different form. That she's now a part of the air, the light, the energy around me. That she's with me in spirit.

They say all of this like it's supposed to help. Like I'm supposed to take comfort in the idea that her presence has turned into some invisible force. That her voice, her laughter, her touch, her habits, her words, can all be replaced with a feeling. As if I should accept absence as a kind of presence.

But I don't feel her. Not even for a second. I don't hear her voice when I need it the most. I don't sense her in the corners of the room. I don't feel any warmth or comfort or signs. I feel the cold silence. I feel the missing routines. I can feel a photo frame that used to be a person. I can feel her last unread message and the thumb-up emoji she sent me for a dish we were supposed to eat together. That is not her presence. That is a wound that never closes.

If she is truly watching, then she is watching me break. Watching me sit in front of a plate of food and not know how to lift the spoon. Watching me share cat reels to her Instagram and then remembering, again and again, that she will never open them. Watching me try not to collapse in front of my father and brother because if I fall apart, we all will. What kind of comfort is that?

They say it so easily. That she's watching. That she's with me. That she wouldn't want to see me like this. But that's not how it feels. She's not watching. She's not here. She's not anywhere. I would trade every made-up spiritual explanation just to hear her call my name once more from the next room.

This house doesn't feel protected. It feels hollow. Her seat is empty. Her bed is untouched. Her voice notes have stopped. Her texts are frozen in time. There's no presence. There's just space that refuses to be filled.

And people say all this is not for me, but for themselves. Because if they admit that she is truly gone, they have to admit that the world is a place where good people can disappear and never return. They want to believe she's with me so they can stay away without feeling guilty. If her spirit is here, then they don't have to be.

But I am not stupid enough to believe that. I know the difference between memory and presence. Between hope and reality. Between silence and her voice.

She's not here. She's not watching. She's gone. And I am alone.

Chapter - 7
You Have to Let Go

They say it softly, like they're offering a warm towel.

"You have to let her go."

As if I'm holding on by mistake. As if continuing to love her is the reason I'm in pain as if the pain itself is wrong. But I never asked to let go. I never agreed to this. I never signed up for a life where letting go was even a question.

She was not a memory to release. She was my mother.

She was the voice in every part of my life.

She was the first person I told anything to, even the smallest things.

She was the only one who made the world feel like it made sense.

Now they want me to let go. Of what? The voice notes I still replay just to hear her? The videos we used to send each other? The messages that stopped mid-conversation? The memory of her waiting for me to come downstairs for lunch? The rituals we had, the food we planned, the reels we laughed at together?

They act like holding on is the problem. But holding on is the only thing keeping me alive.

They expect me to release her like a balloon into the sky. They call that healing. They say that's how I'll find peace. But that kind of peace looks like forgetting. That kind of peace looks like pretending she was just one chapter in my life. But she wasn't a chapter. She was the whole story.

Letting go feels like betrayal. It feels like saying, "I'm okay with you being gone." But I'm not. I'll never be. She didn't let go of me when I was at my worst. She didn't let go when things got difficult. She stayed. And now, in her absence, the only thing I know how to do is stay with her memory. They think letting go makes me strong. I think it makes me hollow. I think it makes me forget why I kept going in the first place. If being strong means abandoning her memory, I don't want that kind of strength.

She is still everything. And I will not let her fade quietly so other people can sleep better.

People think pain is something to be removed. They talk about healing like it's a duty.

They want me to reach a stage where I can remember her without crying, without shaking, without going silent in the middle of a sentence. They say that's what progress looks like. That one day, the memory will bring only warmth and peace.

But I don't want that day to come.

Because if this pain is the only thing that keeps her real, I'll carry it. I'll protect it. I'll hold it like a secret I never want to lose. Because I'm not ready to let her become soft or faded or quiet. She was happy. She was full. She was fire and discipline and laughter and precision. And if it hurts to remember her that way, then let it hurt.

This pain is not a wound I'm trying to close. It is the last thing I have that connects me to how much she mattered. The more it burns, the more I know she was real. The more it aches, the more I know she lived fully, and that I lived fully because of her. If that ache fades, if it softens, if it becomes tolerable, I'm scared she'll disappear in my mind too. And I can't let that happen.

They call it acceptance. But I don't think I want to accept a world where she isn't here. I don't think I ever will. I've seen people who move on. Who smile at her photo and say, "She's in a better place." Who goes back to their routines and treats her like a beautiful chapter that ended.

I'm not like them. I never will be.

Because this pain reminds me of everything we had. It reminds me that the world once had someone like her in it. That I once had someone like her by my side. That someone fought for me, loved me, taught me, protected me, laughed with me, sat across from me while we discussed things as if time were unlimited. And when I feel that pain, I know I haven't left her behind.

So, no. I don't want to be okay. I don't want to be healed. I don't want to arrive at a version of life where she becomes a memory I can live with. I want her to stay alive through this pain. I want this pain to remain sharp. If it breaks me every day, I'll still carry it. Because she's worth carrying.

And if this is the cost of still feeling her with me, I'll pay it every morning. I'll break a thousand times if it means she doesn't fade from me.

I don't want closure. I want her. And I'll live with the pain. Not because I'm brave.

But because I'd rather hurt and remember her clearly than heal and forget how much she meant to me.

I don't know if I want to finish this book.

Because finishing it would mean I've accepted something I never will.

I come here to write when I can't breathe. When the pain feels like it's splitting my chest open.

I come here because I still don't believe she's gone.

And if I stop writing… if I put the final full stop… then what am I left with? Nothing but silence.

And that silence is louder than death.

Maybe I'll never finish this.

Maybe I'll write it forever.

Because the pain isn't getting smaller.

It's getting heavier.

More familiar. Crueller.

I'm having shortness of breath again.

I'm still waiting to wake up from this dream.

It doesn't make sense.

She was just here. She was just talking to me. Sending me food videos. Making dinner plans. Telling me to get married. Begging me to let her dance at my wedding.

She told me that she's scared that if something happens to her, there will be no one to help with my wedding.

And now she's not here.

And there's no one left.

And I didn't give her what she wanted.

I let her down.

I failed her.

I kept saying "later."

Later for the temple visits.

Later, for those foreign trips, she wanted me to join.

Later, for those moments, I thought we had more of.

Later in life she wanted me to build — with a partner, with a family, with joy.

And now there's no later.

I am sorry, Amma.

I'm so sorry.

I wish I could trade my life for yours.

You deserved so much more.

It should have been me.

It should have been me!

I don't want to go on!

I don't care about anything.

Not this book. Not the future. Not work. Not writing. Not God. Not healing.

I just want your back.

Just one moment.

One hug.

One “Nikhil, eat properly.”

One “Come down, food is ready.”

One, “I’m proud of you.”

Please.

Come back.

Even if for one minute.

Please.

There is no point in living or achieving anything in life if it cannot be shared with you. I am unable to see any upside to living without you being there!

Afterword

I don't know what this is supposed to be. A conclusion? There's nothing to conclude. Nothing is resolved. Nothing is healed. This book didn't end. It just stopped when I didn't have the strength to keep writing.

Every day still hurts. I still forget and remember all over again. I still think she's going to call. I still save things to show her. I still break down over the smallest things, the way light falls on the floor, the smell of something cooking, a video of a cat doing something silly. I still wait for a message that will never come.

Some nights I wake up gasping. Other nights I don't sleep at all. The world outside looks the same, but mine isn't. There's a hole in it that will never close. I can't fix it. I can only describe it. And even then, only in pieces.

I thought if I wrote everything down, maybe I would feel lighter. I don't. I thought maybe it would make sense. It doesn't. What happened was senseless. And cruel. And final.

I was so sure she would come back home.

She didn't.

And I don't know what to do with the rest of my life now. I really don't. There's nothing poetic here. Just absence. Just a silence too loud to bear. Just a body moving because it still can, but without purpose. Without center.

This is not a tribute. This is a scream.

And I'm still screaming.